A Bug's World

Hide with the Ladybugs

By Karen Latchana Kenney
Illustrated by Lisa Hedicker

Content Consultant
Clyde Sorenson, PhD
Professor of Entomology
North Carolina State University

magic wagon

visit us at www.abdopublishing.com

Published by Magic Wagon, a division of the ABDO Group, 8000 West 78th Street, Edina, Minnesota 55439.
Copyright © 2011 by Abdo Consulting Group, Inc. International copyrights reserved in all countries. All rights
reserved. No part of this book may be reproduced in any form without written permission from the publisher.

Looking Glass Library™ is a trademark and logo of Magic Wagon.

Printed in the United States of America, North Mankato, Minnesota.
042010
092010

 THIS BOOK CONTAINS AT LEAST 10% RECYCLED MATERIALS.

Text by Karen Latchana Kenney
Illustrations by Lisa Hedicker
Edited by Amy Van Zee
Interior layout and design by Becky Daum
Cover design by Craig Hinton

Library of Congress Cataloging-in-Publication Data
Kenney, Karen Latchana.
  Hide with the ladybugs / by Karen Latchana Kenney ; illustrated by Lisa Hedicker.
    p. cm. — (A bug's world)
  Includes bibliographical references and index.
  ISBN 978-1-60270-785-6
  1. Ladybugs—Juvenile literature. I. Hedicker, Lisa, 1984- , ill. II. Title.
  QL596.C65K46 2011
  638'.5769—dc22

                  2009052913

Table of Contents

Lovely Ladybugs

Crawl, crawl, crawl. A ladybug looks like a colorful, crawling bump. From the side, it's shaped like half a pea. Then it opens its wings. It's gone in a second.

More than 5,000 kinds of ladybugs crawl and fly around Earth. Ladybugs gather in gardens and forests. They live almost everywhere except for very cold places.

Ladybugs are a kind of beetle. Even males are called ladybugs! Ladybugs are also called lady beetles or ladybird beetles.

5

Growing Ladybugs

In the spring, a female ladybug crawls on the underside of a leaf. She is looking for a safe place to lay eggs. Here, the eggs will be safe from hungry birds or insects flying above.

The mother ladybug lays her eggs. Then she flies away. The tiny, yellow eggs look like shiny jellybeans. A mother ladybug doesn't just lay her eggs anywhere. She chooses a place with lots of tiny bugs called aphids. When the eggs hatch, her young will have plenty to eat.

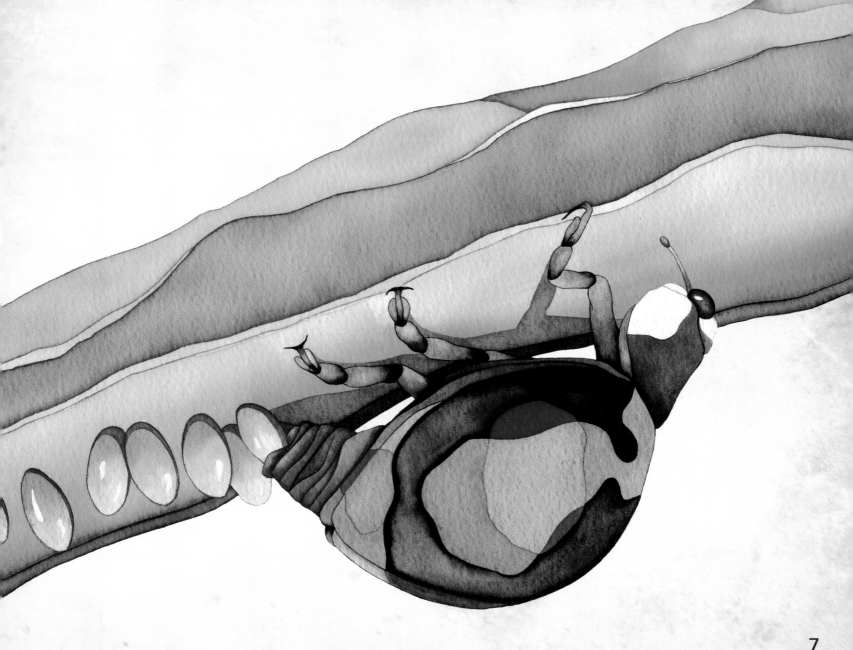

A few days later, larvae hatch from the eggs. These tiny creatures have legs but no wings. They are very hungry! They hunt for aphids.

The larvae are growing quickly. To grow, a larva breaks out of its old skin. Underneath it has new, bigger skin. This is called molting.

A larva can eat 400 aphids before it is three weeks old!

Next, a larva finds a safe place and attaches to a leaf. A hard cover surrounds the larva. It becomes a pupa. Inside the cover, the pupa grows and changes.

Predators might like to eat the pupa. But the pupa's cover looks like bird droppings. This helps the pupa stay safe while it grows.

After a few days, an adult ladybug climbs out of the hard casing. Its body is soft and pale. It does not have spots.

The ladybug's skin soon hardens into a shell. This shell protects the ladybug. Some ladybugs slowly turn red. Their black spots appear.

Ladybugs can be orange, yellow, pink, or black. Some have spots. Some are spotless, and some have stripes.

Flying and Feeling

Soon, ladybugs are flying. Each one has two sets of wings. Unlike other insects, beetles have elytra. The elytra are hard, front wings. They cover a pair of thin, see-through back wings.

To fly, the ladybug opens its front wings. Then the thin wings flutter. They lift the ladybug into the air.

The two elytra are a mirror image of each other. They have the exact same color and spots.

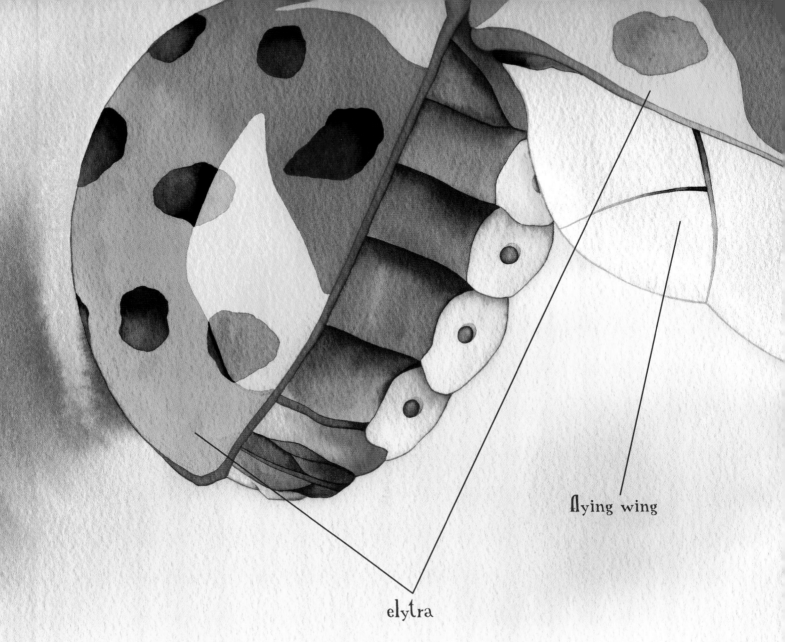

elytra

flying wing

17

Ladybugs cannot see faraway things well. How do they find food?

A ladybug uses its two antennae to explore its world. Like wands, they wave in all directions. They can feel, smell, and taste.

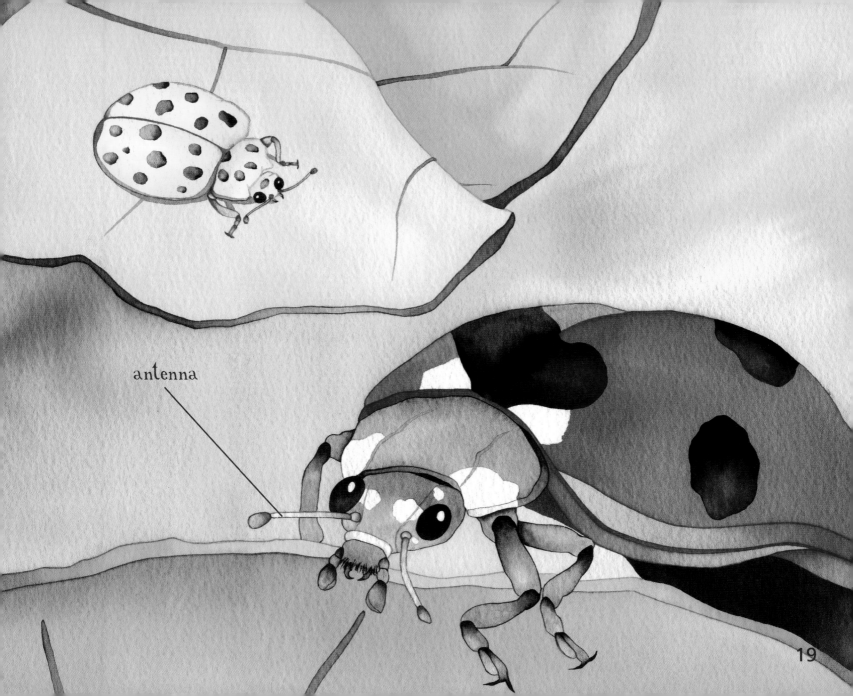

antenna

Helpful Bugs

A ladybug has caught an aphid. Near the ladybug's mouth are two powerful mandibles. It uses these to chew its meal.

Ladybugs eat aphids or scale bugs. These tiny creatures are pests. They harm crops. That's why farmers and gardeners love to see ladybugs crawling around. More ladybugs means fewer pests. An adult ladybug can eat 75 aphids a day! A few kinds of ladybugs eat plant parts. Some eat pollen, the sticky dust on flowers.

The Mexican Bean Beetle and Squash Lady Beetle are two ladybugs that eat plants. Their names tell the plants they eat.

21

Staying Safe

Danger is near! A predator is flying overhead. A ladybug rolls onto its back so it looks dead. The bird isn't interested in eating a dead ladybug.

Ladybugs can also give off a stinky liquid from their bodies. This juice is the insect's blood. It tastes and smells bad. Predators stay away.

The air has a chill. Winter is coming. Ladybugs find a dry place away from the wind. It can be in a house or in a dead tree. Sometimes, they form large groups.

The ladybugs stay there through winter. They do not eat anything. They could stay like this for nine months.

Most ladybugs live for about a year, but some live longer.

New Lives

When the air is warm again, the ladybugs go back outside.
They fly around the garden. They hunt for aphids. The females
lay eggs. New ladybugs begin their lives.

A Ladybug's Body

A ladybug's body has three main parts: the head, the thorax, and the abdomen. The ladybug does not have bones. Instead, a hard casing covers its body like a suit of armor.

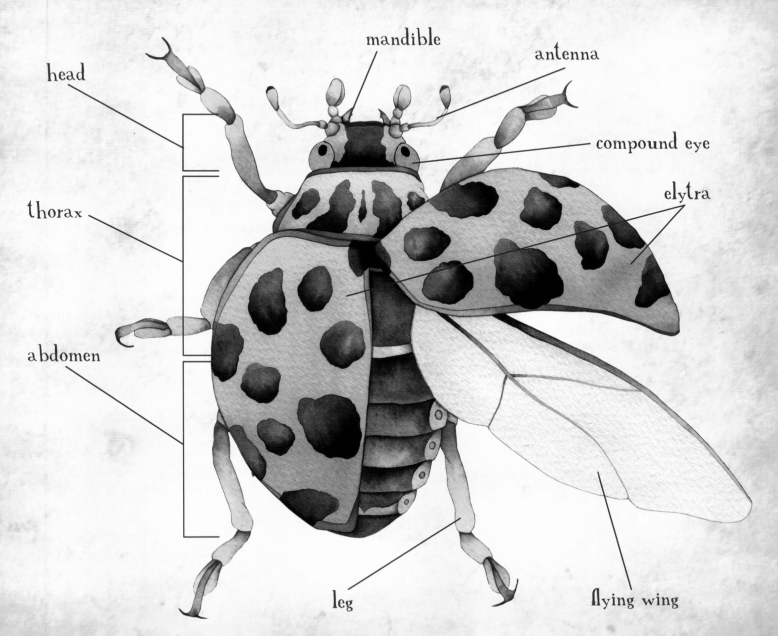

head

mandible

antenna

compound eye

elytra

thorax

abdomen

leg

flying wing

29

A Closer Look

Spots and Colors

What you will need:

- picture of an Ashy Gray Lady Beetle
- picture of a Pink Spotted Lady Beetle
- notebook paper
- pencil

There are many kinds of ladybugs on Earth. They come in different colors. They also have different spots or none at all.

Look at the pictures of the two different ladybugs. Draw two boxes on a piece of paper. Write "Ashy Gray" at the top of one box. Write "Pink Spotted" at the top of the other box. Write about each ladybug.

- What color is it?
- What do the spots look like?
- What size is it?

Then write about the ways the ladybugs are different from each other.

Ladybug Facts

- A ladybug beats its wings **85** times each second when it flies.
- Ladybugs have been to space on a shuttle! Scientists wanted to know how ladybugs would act without the pull of Earth. They watched the ladybugs catch and eat aphids.

Glossary

abdomen—the back part of an insect's body.

antenna (an-**TEH**-nuh)—one of the two long, thin body parts that sticks out from an insect's head and is used to feel and smell.

aphids—small bugs that eat parts of plants.

elytra—the hard wings of a beetle.

mandibles—the jaws of a bug.

molt—to break out of a layer of skin so that new, bigger skin can grow.

pollen—a fine, yellowish powder released from flowers.

scale bugs—small bugs that eat parts of plants.

thorax—the middle part of an insect's body.

On the Web

To learn more about ladybugs, visit ABDO Group online at **www.abdopublishing.com**. Web sites about ladybugs are featured on our Book Links page. These links are routinely monitored and updated to provide the most current information available.

Index